SPLITTING THE HEART

To
Helen,
Mermaid Love
Happy Holidays!
Janet Rogers
12/07

SPLITTING THE HEART

JANET MARIE ROGERS

Library and Archives Canada Cataloguing in Publication

Rogers, Janet Marie, 1963-
Splitting the heart / Janet Rogers.

Poems.
ISBN 978-1-897430-04-0

1. Indians of North America--Canada--Poetry. 2. Indian women--Canada--Poetry.
I. Title.

PS8585.O395198S69 2007 C811'.6 C2007-903687-2

Cover art: Janet Marie Rogers, "The Storytellers"
Cover photo: Eagle Eye Pictures © 2007

Published in 2007 by:
Ekstasis Editions Canada Ltd.
Box 8474, Main Postal Outlet
Victoria, B.C. V8W 3S1

Ekstasis Editions
Box 571
Banff, Alberta T0L 0C0

Splitting the Heart has been published with the assistance of grants from the Canada Council for the Arts and the British Columbia Arts Council administered by the Cultural Services Branch of British Columbia.

CONTENTS

SPLITTING THE HEART

I AM BOTH

I am strong
like bloody
iron and steel

I am mighty
I am sister
to the grand mountains
overlooking the land
generation after
generation
after generation

I AM
Sky Woman
plummeting fast
through the air
in complete trust
into the arms
of my people

I am so strong
I make strong people
feel empowered

my power feeds the
solid air waves
sending encouraging messages
out to the masses
touching far reaches
of every territory

and I stand
with the bravest
of warriors
in defense
and in defiance

I raise my voice
in love and in song
to praise the powers
that came before me

I embrace truth
like a long lost
relation
finding the way back home

I am all these things
singularly and all together

because I know
who I am

I am
a strong
Indian
woman

and

I am tired and timid
I have the shame
of seven generations
running through my veins

I have not learned
to turn off the tortured
voices telling me lies
and I will not try
I will not be myself
because I don't know
who that is

I have no strength
to defend myself
I worry every minute

about a future that may not be

I HATE
my brothers and sisters
because they don't
know how to live
I do not believe my culture
will save me
it has no place in this life

I am a fake
I mistake kindness
and am suspicious of it
I don't keep promises
especially to myself

I expect the smallest
amounts of everything
and I am willing
to beg for it

I am weakened by my addictions
and sickened by the addictions
that keep my people weak

I will not tell the truth
and I accept my right
to remain silent
I will hide my true blood
and do everything to
blend in because
I don't
care
I
am
an
Indian
woman

FLOAT

the trick is
to stay airborne
lifted
even when
restless winds
rest
stay lifted

work with
and against
gravity's invisible
laws

resist

your own desire
to descend
be the migrating
butterfly
find your personal
thermal
and fly

keep flying

this is not
a test
forget
your safety net
it won't help
to prove
your will

do all you can

stay lifted

THREE DAYS WITH YOU(S)

reading your poetry
made me want to write
my poetry
not understanding
what you said
but liking the way
you said it

all the   *talk talk talk*
about   *art art art*
a smorgasbord

I gorged myself
and went to bed late

three days of the same faces
anonymous, oblivious
to the love we were cultivating
vibrating inside
us all

seeing your art
made me wanna
put down my brush
change my pallet from
grey   to   black

we gathered in the back
of thick-walled rooms
facing unfinished canvasses
building to a crescendo
increasing in volume
with every new stroke

in this room
we are equals
equally blessed
our gifts forced into corners
lightning in the dark

watching you perform
made me want to stop talking
adopt the language of action
and say deep things
I know won't be understood

playing with props   building blocks

touch – look away
touch – look away

sitting beside you
made me want to
stay there
recognizing the skin
the hair
defining us like geography
I'll be the river
you be the mountain
you be the canyon
and *you* be the sun scorched plains

we'll make a place
for love
for the Indians
coming up
and for those who came before

in the end, we become
hungry brown birds
necks lurched upward
mouths at the ready
feeding on heat waves

tons of fun
an auditorium full of half-breeds
makes one damn big Indian

for the finale
we'll learn to swim in the tears
not drown
climb out of pain
not sink
we'll feed our masks
and learn our songs
play a bone game
where rules don't exist
and everybody wins

STORY: TIME

for Victoria E.

my stories are weary
from the long journey
through ancestral time
standing tall   telling all
of my people
who we are
what we've become

humiliation
through the years
the deaf ears
stripped of original dress
decorated in drag
lost and researched
brought-back bits
of broken translations
story poetry
spinning clues
syllable food
for hungry souls
constantly craving

Who am I?

lends reason to why
we watch endless hours
of television stories
bend our ears to radio waves
violently crack the spines
of forgiving books
and pay with attention
to readers
reciting in character voice
their history
all relative   realistically
intertwining our lives

relating to strangers
on the screen
on the page
the stage

hundreds   thousands
millions of stories
layered on top
untold histories
beneath our feet
resting
escaping excavation

this is my story
as tired and watered down
as it is
as torn and manipulated
as it has become
a cocktail of a story
mixed and shaken
with a twist of humour
to help it go down

proud pride
without innocence
clinging to colours
of my people
hoping their knowing
will rub off

I bring my kindling stories
to their rich fires
cast a new light
reveal wall writings
telling in pictures
who they were
equals
who I am
today

JUST TRY

it was like
a fall day in Maine
crisp and crystal clear
liquid light pouring into me
monumental mental messages
of understanding

it was like
Leonard Cohen saying
Pass me a pen, I want to
write something down
it was that profound
the understanding

I am North American

yes, we say *No* to the border
dotted lines separating
pushing us up and over
distance and time

I am North American

no more an angry Indian
I am content in my disgust
I like that you don't trust me
and think that I have everything

it makes me try harder
not to barter my way through
so to begin I'll win
this North American idol
of poetry

filing acts of civil disobedience
cleaning up the mess

no more talks *this*
is my road block *these*
are my lines *this*
is my line
cross it
just try
come over to my side
just try

befriend me
be an ally
look through my glasses
walk in my shoes
eat at my table
one day
just one day

just try

you can see who I am
on the status card
that took six years to get
and the passport
I have to renew yet
and still the questions come…

Where are you from?
What is your citizenship?

I'll tell you
my citizenship
if you tell me
the name of the ship
your people
came over on

I think this
and they let me go on

I am North American
not to be confused with
Canadian the beverage
I haven't drank in sixteen years
tell that to the beer company
pimping out its country
in the name of sales

wait a minute
I'm not quite done
this is all in fun
so if I've offended you *relax*
this is not an attack on you
I'm just spilling my truth
living proof
that a Mohawk goddess
warrior poet
still screams like E. Pauline

home-girl pioneer
hip- hop- scotching a rhythmic
trail from Missouri
to Alaska from Victoria
to Boston
and beyond

she made this land
her literary playground
and I intend to do the same
without blame
pointing fingers
or instilling guilt
that's not what my power is built on

So
my name may get bigger
and I'd still be the nigger
of this land
now do you understand how it works?

I AM HOME

I am home
south of the border
and south of that border

everywhere is home
everyplace is sacred
Indigenous land

the minute you think you own it
that's when you've blown it

people old as the trees
can be found
standing this ground
we're a package deal

I am
the North American messenger
and gladly
pay the price
to bring these words to you
cuz
you can't sue
someone who has nothing
to lose

go ahead
just try

WITHOUT HUMAN PRESSURE

I am waiting
to be shown
who I am
for a new perspective
to clear away
questions
for my reflection
to speak back
answers
and say
this way   is your way

I'm waiting for
road signs
that say
only ten more miles to go
almost there
but not quite
I'm waiting for
state troopers
to bust me
make me start again

I'm waiting
to sleep with Creator
give me pleasure
without human pressure
to re-start my heart
quick
cuz I'm sick
of waiting

I'm still waiting
for adolescence
to pass
for my skin to clear
for life to begin after forty
find that special someone
settle down
do things

I'M WAITING

I'm on the road waiting
for the parade to begin
hearing the band
off in the distance
playing songs
I can't wait
...to sing...

...still waiting...

GONE NOW

the teapot is empty
while shades of night and day
transport shadows
across the kitchen floor

spiky thorns were more your cup
and mine was fruit-flavoured leaves
yet all the minutes in a year
could not steep from you
the words I longed to hear

faded curtains swing the
lazy rhythm of summer breezes
letting light in briefly
barely blocking harsh glare

the reality of our union
covers me now
like an itchy blanket
and wish I didn't miss
the things about you
through the years I grew to despise
the many lies

all is not lost though you are gone now
the lines of survival
like war-paint decorate my face
and the boy and girl
grown
gone

the grass yellow and uneven
calls to me from beyond
a creaky porch floor

gone now

THAT REMINDS ME

he reminds me   of you
in the gruff
whiskey tone
of his voice
in the dark
mysteries
behind his eyes
he reminds me   of you
the way
you moved
the way you
devoured
your interests
by the handfuls
never bothering to chew

does she remind you   of me
in anyway
does she collect
all your doubts
drown them out
do magic tricks
all the while   smiling

Does she?

introduce you
to trust and love
unconditional
warrior values
we learned
and knew   does she
dress in blue   chiffon
and dance a slow
hula for you

I'd do that again
in a heartbeat

he brings me blossoms
and chocolates
tries to prove
he is good
while *we* never
passed empty words
to one another
always aware
the gifts we shared
were delicate and brief

real

as flesh on fire

COMING HOME

miles
separate us
memory
touch

I'm coming home
shy in my skin
unsure
of what waits
pleasure?
shame?

tomorrow
separates us
my home
does not know me
now
it does not
welcome me back
but is
congenial
as a guest

my bones
have sunk too deep
into footpaths
leading away
towards
territories
and extended families
accepting me in

BACK STROKE

my soul sank
deep into the blood
of this land
I extended a hand
looking for help
sinking fast   back
into history
time traveling
through layers
to the core

an innocent beginning

swam in the sweat
of my ancestors
back stroked
my way
to safety
a time
of strength
without racism
and floated there

basking in liquid love

skin love
Indian love
so true
so real
shaking your belief
in anything
less

RE(D)CYCLE

I love this skin
Creator put me in
so attractive to the eye
equal to the landscape
perfect against the sky
I'll leave my skin
when I am gone
to a drum maker I know
have him tie me
on a thick round frame
paint tiny flowers round
all the same

from my bones
he'll fashion sticks
also wrapped in skin
and beat out songs
of my history
Grandmother stories and medicines

hold fast to me
the flesh drum
feel me tighten
against your warmth
hang me by the fire at night
I'll creek and yawn till dawn

from my skull
carve a rattle
powerful and strong
shake out
old memories
in pictures words and song

use my hair as fringe
on your coat
it too holds
knowledge of things

fasten it with fingerbone buttons
against winter winds that sting

my teeth   use for gambling
they'll win you a big pot
blow them with a magic breath
take care you don't get caught

trade my ribs for anything you need
but keep for yourself, the extra one
with it make a whistle for dance
when you gather neath the sun

these human gifts
I ask you use
to heal the sick
or simply amuse
then burn the rest
to feed the crops
and see this cycle
never stops

re(d) cycle

THIS IS REAL

his answers are there
beneath the bark
between tight grains
behind discoloured skin
striking metal to wood
peeling in fevered rips
towards the reward
the shape – the stories – the newborn you

a mask   to play the part
a plaque   to represent
a bowl   to hold your own
and a rattle…

to call it all in

scripture grains decoded by touch
teach him histories
never taught or told
holds tightly to tools
gains control
watching chips fall
where they may
swept away for tomorrow…

more wood forms
grow from his hands
details reveal secrets
to the the artist   he's earned
in creation time

all is clear
peace prevails

THIS IS REAL

compared to confusion
surrounding him outside
where worlds collide
and clashshshshshshsh

a man and his tools
hands heart and mind
find the way

his answers are there…

MAKE ME

he makes me naked
and takes me
under his skin
holds me in his bloodstream
letting me have a taste

he makes me feel
all warm and fuzzy
cuz he knows
what I like
I paddle my way
to his heart
feel it start to palpitate
knowing he will hate
himself for loving me

he makes me moan
a song
not sung
in quite some time
he knows the rhyme
and together we make
harmony

I tap his spine
with a spike and a pail
harvest sweet
sap
and save it for later
when I am alone
running low
on his sticky elixir
bath in it *drink it down*
this love
we have found

I make him naked
see his secrets
so exposed
straight to the bone

I take him
into my lungs
breathe him
in
and
out

hold him in my throat
make him tickle
when I laugh
and when we do the math
two
can't be divided

by anything

When he says
Love me

I say
Make me

ONE WOMAN PARADE

enter plasma pink
cocktail foam
wafts of cologne
stronger than repellent
enter glamour and confidence
aged beauty head to toe
mostly gray   brown roots
give way to fusia coloured shoots
done up in a bun

A month in the sun
she claims is better
than the chiropractor
pupils dulled and small
between furry framed lash
clinging to lids half mast
boobs   tired   overworked
served her well back in the day
she prays they stay in place
shaped by wire and lace

one woman parade

promenades her way
to town
never mind what they say
she's earned this
liberation
her freedom to be

eccentric ending
to a life lived well
only she can tell
how much it cost

THAT'S WHY...

it is the most powerful
most potent
most profound
thing I can do
I write...

it is in my bones
and soul
that I do so

I write because
I can
am able
to incite change
exercise my free will
write what I want
because others
cannot

I write to pay homage
to the twilight hours
affording me time
for the brightness
of day
when I see
with clear eyes and mind
the genius or foul gifts
delivered at night

it makes an eco-system of me
pen paper artist word
I write from the inside
out of control
no doubt to cloud the cause
to tell me I can't or shouldn't
or this is *bullshit*

I write to encourage others
to do the same –
you're just as good
start with a word
make it meaningful and true
keep it fresh and new
just keep writing

like taking a train
'til it transports you
stopping and starting
clickity-clack   click

I write to remember
I write because I have
lazy ears
I write to see
if it can be done
I write to reach you
I write to calm
my twitchy itchy digits
it's what I do

Do you?

I'm the guy
hunched over a
worn torn journal
scratching illegible secrets
in a coffee shop
nursing espresso # 3
cuz I know it bugs you

I can't help it

I have to

I write
its the only useful thing
I learned in school
I write and that makes
actors speak   without me
the stage would be silent

it all begins with the word

I write about rain
about land
I write from the twisted
sick depths of my broken
heart
wax poetic about
past lovers
and spin wishes
into reality
spells
broken down
tucked inside stone
left to disintegrate
at a natural rate
like watching
warm words
turn to vapour
spoken into icy air

I write with a pen
and again I wonder
what they did before
how did they record
the angst-filled history
and re-written truths?

oral evidence
cannot live in tight-lipped libraries
no index card for reference
it sits – out there
vulnerable to interpretation and change
inside our tiny little brains

write them down
your confessions
and alibis
don't believe everything
you read
trust how the words
hit you

how are you?
Fine
and you?

I write left-handed
down from three
generations ago
people I don't know
who tell me
to write

in dreams they come
and fill my pen
with medicine
wait   patient
until I approach the page
to attack
its like crack

I'm addicted
(if there's a cure for this, I don't want it)

my passion is pure
like thick black ink
oozing fast-rapid lines
of honesty
I can hardly keep up
wait for me…

the movement so swift
this gift   never a curse
it'd be worse
not to go
with the flow
cuz   now I know

now I know

now I know

what it means
to be in the zone
alone   and yet not
remembering what I forgot

these words are my
birthright
I write them
therefore I am

FREE

WATCH YOUR STEP

could be the ancient stone
standing as constant witness
or the crisp quality of
mountain air
or the jutting slate
landing strip
for star cousins

...Coyote is here

swinging his bulging bag of tricks
whispering suggestive suggestions
to the wind
decorating trees with ribbon
reflecting him

...he watches

as we make attempts   fail
make attempts   fail
eggs on fate

hold fist fights
battle royal to the death
Coyote knows defeat is temporary
continues his dance
black eyes bloody nose and all
carries himself proud
tail swishing
enticing the younger less learned
to worship him

Coyote sings loud
frightens Elk annoys Crow
and recedes back into stone
takes on new shapes
flattens down to brown
earth beneath our feet
loyal to his post

his mission?
to trip us
up

YOUR MEDICINE

for our youth

the medicine of you
clings to me
it brings me
warm memories
of true moments
lived in creativity
lit up
with ruby hearts
beating in perfect time

the medicine we made
flipped on
like a light
our feelings were right
on the surface
ready to serve us
in dance   in song
prayer   and sharing

the medicine of your mind
blew mine
away
like bullets flying stray
striking places
we didn't know
were wounded

a reunion
of heart   spirit   thought
we taught
each other
with tenderness
and patience

Did you really need
my direction
to get you
where you already were?

I wasn't sure

your bright lights
are so blinding
it's heartening
to know
our future art
is in your hands

take a stand
take your light
turn to the left
and turn to the right
the medicine in you
is brewed
in collective cauldrons
long ago
feeding the blood
like honey
in the veins

you are the future
of what is
heavy responsibility
granted to those
who can shoulder
the burden

It's curtain
take the stage

INDIAN SEX

tones of tanned flesh
pressed together   long black hair
twisted   tangled between   fingers
red tongues exposed   then hidden
dark eyes squeezed hard
shut tight
animal movement caught
in moonlight

howling and growling
sounds of rustling   thrusting
panting   breathing
hearts beating
dangerous pleasures
a scratch   a bite
strong fingers hold tight

two potent people
power creatures
come together
above
the lovers   wild rattles
and singers scream

Indian sex   makes
nature smile
whirlwinds fly
paints the sky
pink   orange
dusty sweat bleeds
from every pore
energy transforms
clouds begin to cry
cleansing   blessing
natural acts
satisfied

SWIMMING

I call it swimming
as you dive into me
float through me

I call it swimming
as you stroke my hair
shake it loose like seaweed
make me your mermaid

still you swim
rapid laps around me
leaving rumpled linen
in your wake

holding your breath
you approach the surface
treasures gathered from the deep
held in your teeth

swim a marathon with me
to exhaustion
battling rough seas
and fatigue
to claim our prize

I call it swimming

dive in

INDIAN LOVE

Indian love
starts with a giggle
hand over mouth
and warm red cheeks
Indian love
moves like a river
passing over pebbles
singing liquid songs

Indian love
feels like warm fry bread
and smells
like fresh sage
Indian love
tickles like feathers
making big bellies shake
brown smiles grow wide

Indian love
is shared like food
enough for all
no matter how small

Indian love
heals you
like a warm winter fire
on a cold wet night

Indian love
looks like elders
lined-faced
kind-eyed elders

Indian love
tastes like soda pop
bubbly burping
honey-sweetened soda pop

Indian love
stings when lost
like bees angry and sore
Indian love
transcends time

...the proof is in our presence

CHECK POINT

another day
young ones wait outside
without coats
without kisses goodbye
for late buses
to take them
to racist schools

the girl who
rings my groceries through
has scars on her wrists
and wishes me a
Good day

the English say
they like this city best
because it has no blacks

I save food I cannot finish
for a man leaning
on the restaurant window
then goes awkward
into the night

hallways host the portrait
of a past leader
conveniently forgetting
his heritage
teachers not found guilty
continue to take
students to bed

my mother gives me an
afghan woven with
magic and protection
to use everyday
nature's disasters
make war on us
as we war
with one another

the television is telling me
I'll never be pretty enough
and the men believe it

we buy
genetically modified food
and couples keep
reproducing

the Grandmothers
go to jail for protecting
their land
setting the example again
for the rest of us

warriors choose
to die accepting defeat
willingly giving their lives
breaking hearts
keeping promises

the Eagle's timing
is always perfect
appearing overhead
delivering hope

prisons are full
of fathers and brothers
learning to exist
in abnormality

poets keep writing
long long verses
of strength and survival
on paper they find
in bins

sometimes I fantasize
about murder
and lighting a candle in a church for you

the families return
to food banks
loaded down with emptiness
on the way home

the fire keeps us warm
at night
heating our dreams
easing our sleep
before another day
begins

some have the luxury
of education
and I have liberation
in the absence of it

we struggle to define love
rather than wait
for it to drop clues
marked skin
of butterflies
and cheery things
cannot tell me
who you are

I will return
to the forests
and wait
for you there
protecting a place
for the future

RECIPE FOR THE FUTURE

she is only half
half of her father
who is whole
nothing of her mother
who is none
but oh so much more
than a whole bunch
put together

Half – 0.5 – 1 over 2

looking into the mirror
she poked at her reflection
Only half
she whispered
she pulled out
all the portrait photos
of herself
and cut them down the centre
Only half
she stated

she contemplated
the government-issued card
used to keep count
and keep out
Half enough
she announced

it wasn't that she was incomplete
it wasn't that there was something
missing
she is the new hybrid
she is the shade of the future
her blood red
her skin brown
her pride full

half of nothing – is nothing
she is half of something
the half cup of tasty ingredients
mixed in mysterious kitchens

she is only half
because any more than half
would spoil the recipe

HIGH HEELS

like a cat
coming home
after a long   hard night
she treads through sidewalks
thick with bad breath
looking like gold

a fluffy feather boa
slinks along beside
bushy faced men
sneak a pinch from behind
she slaps them hard
then runs away in play

she sings old French songs
she learned as a child
gesturing with long
expressive fingers
lingering from her
feminine form   *tres petite*

they whistle   when she passes
she lives for this
her scent is strong
like her accent
luring them close
she invites them to
enjoy her
take in her softness

Regarde! – she is woman

she curses high heels
slowing her
on low busy streets
prancing along
in painful elegance
making men wait   and they wait
her pussycat smiles
disguise claws
sharp as razors
wit   quick as silver
a gaze that can cut
to your very soul

she is woman – *Regarde*!

SHE REMEMBERS

she visits
the land
of others
walks
with the Grandfathers
those who offered
help when she lived there

she sits
and listens
while the ocean
sings its song
along with Raven
and his brothers

the sun shifts
in an active sky
painting quick
shadows
on hand-carved totems
standing tall as
church steeples
on a grassy plain

she touches
the wooden skin
breathes them in
feels waves inside
connect to her hand
...she understands

she whispers her story
she cries at the foot
...and she remembers

QUOTES OF THE HEART

I.

I would not pretend
to be someone I'm not
to make you love me
for fear
you may love
the illusion
more than me

II.

I thought I felt
a menstrual cramp
like my tubes
squeezing closed
though I did not bleed
it was just a memory
of long ago

III.

touch me
caress me
bend me
burn me
then fear me
oh yes
fear me

IV.

we placed our rings
in a glass bowl
covered them with sand
till they fused
into one

V.

when I call
your name
in the forest
do you hear
anything?

VI.

wine me
dine me
just don't do
your Elvis
impression

VII.

we sang beautifully
together
until
the band stopped

VIII.

my cat
and your dog
look like
John and Yoko

IX.

lunching with Sasquatch
I reached for the berries
heard a loud grumble
and waited for them
to be passed

X.

fortunate
coincidences
can be trickster's way
of playing

GOOD SAVAGE

be a good savage
tell us your secrets
write them all down
so we'll remember
share them with the world
given permission
or not

be a good savage
dance and sing for us
as we marvel at your culture
see the whole show for free
then walk away

be a good savage
string us some beads
tokens of our encounter
surely you need the change
to pay for the addictions
that we gave you

be a good savage
remain ignorant of the rules
to the game
of land claim and inherent rights
no one likes a smart Indian
that's not part of who you are

be a good savage
become one of us
reject your community
your families your homes
because you're just like us anyway

be a good savage
speak only when spoken to
sit at our table
sign our papers
then disappear

be a good savage
forget what my ancestors
did to your ancestors
let's break bread, drink wine
heck, let's even interbreed
mixed bloods make beautiful children

be a good savage
just sit tight
as we vote away your rights
wash our hands of the Indian problem
surely you understand

be a good savage
and just don't say
a word

EXPERIMENTAL PERSPECTIVES I

honesty
is the natural state
of the universe
while
abundant lessons
on how to unlearn it
await round every corner

abundance
is the natural state
of the universe
while river beds
once thick and fast
trickle softly
and whisper songs
once roared

compassion
is the natural state
of man
yet we adopt unnatural rules
so cruel
and condemn others
as if we wrote them
ourselves

beauty
is the natural state
of all physical life
so why do we worship
prototypes
and convince ourselves
that we do not fit?

curiosity
is the natural state
of human beings
call it exploration
experimentation
or trial and error
it's how we learn
it is our inspirational
motivation to all things
new

productivity is
the natural state of nature
resistance to inertia
serving a purpose
through work
reproducing producers
productive is our state of being
perpetuating our purpose
to serve

companionship
relationships
we want and need this
natural as breath to birth
we connect
and reject
and connect again
seeing ourselves in others
and others in someone else

EXPERIMENTAL PERSPECTIVES II

confusion
is evil
its missing bits
of information
withheld deliberately
causing self-doubt
makes us debate
our happiness
and sanity
this disease
spun from
dishonesty

intelligence
is action separate
from our heart's desires
the practice of science
and things
easy to define
different from wisdom
and of equal value
a learned virtue
sometimes a blessing
from above

happiness
is knowing
who you are
and knowing your right
to defend who you are
at all times
seeing you
be yourself   with me
knowing our unity
is born form
honesty

love is BEING
listening to silence
content in our skin
knowing we are
the very thing
that Created us
in love

creation
is plucking elements
from thin air
combined
with intelligence
love   clarity   experience
to produce
a unique contribution
something close
to nature

fear
is absence of faith
feeling unable
to overcome
unfamiliar circumstances
believing
you are not free
to exercise choice
apply will
a paralyzing fallacy

understanding
is knowing
your purpose
so every deed
done with intention
reflects truth

hope
is realizing
you are powerless
and still anticipating
favourable   desirable outcomes
it is the coin tossed –
waiting to see
how it lands

wealth
is found
in things that cannot be traded
it is our birthright
the songs inside you
sung in the face
of your enemy

SEX SHAMAN

sensual ritual
lines drawn in the sand
crossed over hand in hand
whale oil light
casts quivering mounds
breech through shadows
like newborns on all fours
simultaneous
tears and laughter
of extraordinary pleasures
mixing fluids with sap
back into blood
pools in eyes
easily rise
whispering undetectable dialect
soft suggestions
unable to disobey
sex shaman songs
shared through breath exchange
hyper-ventilate swoon movement
hypnotic trance duality dance
sewing sex parts together
sister to brother versa-vise
cum by northern lights
swollen by southern tonics
beguiled by western darkness
eastern morning brings
quiet disorientation
suspended disbelief
relief skin presence
physical existence
sweat beads strung
stinging lungs
initiation incantation

love

REFLECTIONS

history
reflective
shared in collective stories
spoken remembrances
of token gifts
given   and taken away

our lineage is long
with names
coming
down
from   names
we are made of these names
family braids
thick as rope
pull us along
bring us up
save us
from drowning
in anonymous
seas

For aaaaall generations
For aaaaall generations

we call him Uncle
and in our relation
equation
it adds up
they call me Sister
biologically incorrect
makes us reflect
on family

generations to be
rise like sparks
reproducing
perpetuating
reasons to gather fuel
for future fires

WE are the people
who make the families,
who build the communities,
who dance in
our future

living   breathing
cultural faces
reflective faces
of Grand People's love
for
yesterday   tomorrow
and today

For aaaaall generations
For aaaaall generations

THIS HISTORY

this history
you say is mine
well
I have to question it
put it under a light
and examine it
study every detail
for flaws
to see if it resembles
anything
close to mine

I'll show you
my truth
then you show me
proof
that I should adopt
your perspective
on how you think
we have won this
age long battle

because

history is always
written by victors
and your stories
are written in a language
you assume
not mine

pardon me
if I contradict
your education
it is my obligation
to share
ancestral memory
unfiltered
and unafraid
bring your words
into light
from their deep
dark ceded homes
to give you

a choice

your history
versus
my reality
in the match
of the centuries

for one must die

in my books
there's only room
for truth

GETTING HERE

hit the road
on the boat
load land
on the other side

crossing over…

visiting The House of Bees
collecting pollen medicine
ease my fever
cursing my cool
helping me heal
sensing you
riding inside
my head and heart
you departed
from this earth
but did not leave me
I see why
I am returning
to the place we last were
giving back the tears
that began here
and put our journey to rest

It took so long getting here

every song played
spoke of our pain
purged me of my hurt
emptied all the darkness
you introduced to me
of a time that used to be
and soon will be no more

I am here now
and you hitched a ride here too
I feel you everywhere
perhaps you came to say
hello/goodbye
to the land
revisit your clan
before you continue on…

when I go
please don't follow
my road is different
a gift
returned and deserved
knowing happiness
can be mine
you left me behind
to live a good life for you
to breathe as you would
and pray as you did
for all our greater good

It took so long getting here

BEING INDIAN

being Indian takes more than having a status card stuffed in your wallet
it takes jabs to the heart
in the face too once or twice

it takes brown skin so the white race can judge you
it takes a strong spirit born of humility
and the ability to withstand more of the same

it takes love
love of community to feel blessed when surrounded by your people
to be part of your survivor race

it takes a sense of responsibility
to the brown youth, to instill pride
stand as an example while you look to *your* elders
as a measure of *your* path

it takes poverty in the pocket to use that Ingin-nuity
it takes stories, lots and lots and lots of stories

it takes rough skin and bad breath, it takes scars and blood
it takes knowing your songs, old, old songs sung in your language
with drums and rattles and dancers moving in clockwise
and counter clockwise circles   *can you see it?*

it takes belly laughs and dry humour
it takes that innate bingo gene – we've all played at least once.

it takes animals visiting your dreams
speaking to your spirit, silent messages of encouragement or warning

it takes gratitude for everything everyday – I'm not even kidding
it takes alcoholism and abuses of every kind
racial abuse   sexual abuse   and most importantly   self-abuse

BEING INDIAN TAKES MORE

it takes hate
it takes growing out of that hate into calm stoic acceptance
it takes beautiful eyes   pitch black beads

it takes more than sporting jewelry dangling obvious around your neck
it takes stomachs lined with grease and flour
empty of foods that feed our bodies.
being Indian is more than a word
it's a way of life

I think like an Indian
he walks like an Indian
we breed like Indians
because
we like sex   we're good at it

it takes fatherless children
whose knowledge of their fathers is sketchy at best
it takes a wise Indian to refuse pedestals
to choose our battles carefully

BEING INDIAN TAKES MORE

it takes millions of staff
to keep us in count
had enough?
too bad
being Indian takes getting in your face and staying there
till more Indians come or the cops arrive
usually in that order

it takes tear drops as big and as many to fill the Grand Canyon

being Indian is a full time job
there's no such thing as a weekend Indian
it takes forms and records
it takes cheques and grants
it takes turning those grants into beautiful Indian art
that lives in museums
as tangible evidence
of our hard-earned existence

it takes gatherings and powwows   feasts   and potlatches
It takes going home

BEING INDIAN TAKES MORE

being Indian means **BEING INDIAN**
not First Nations Aboriginal or Indigenous –
there's a difference

being Indian takes lies and the truth
and instincts as strong as rock
to know the difference

being Indian takes anger and adoption
it takes removal and memories
loss of memories

it takes denial
denial of identity
as you walk past a longhaired brother begging for change
you think
that's not me   guess again

being Indian takes literacy
the ability to read clouds
and signals of smoke
dissemination of belts in beads
invitations of wampum

it takes
AAAAAAAAALLLLLLLLL
my relations
without hesitation
to answer the call

being Indian takes more…

that's all

ALL MAPPED OUT

lined up
between
flimsy leaves
I see
family
anthropology
offers no apology
for the tortured images
and badly written
histories
sour trades
made
between pages
of my people
telling me tales
I find hard
to believe

posed
there against
unclaimed
landscapes
bravely displayed
they look away
towards
unsure futures
tele-transported
through time

I find
new relations
beyond the frame
behind the lens
and friends
who want the same
posed *our numbers grow*
how quickly we forget
making it easy
to steal
our soul

turn the page
to find people
of the plains
fine feathered families
stories told in shades
of black and white and grey
leather textured
kin

first contact begins
spoken history
replaced by
paper

in the index
we are listed
from Abanaki
to Yakima
with highbred
and sub-breeds
everything in between

we need
new encyclopedias
with creative descriptions
and maps to include
displacement
it's funny
these categories
miss the story
completely

re-writing comes easy
removal breaking our links
abstract as mathematics
printed in ink
to make it true

A TRIP THROUGH PARADISE

we take
earthquake rides
over rock waves
kissing
lake faces
stretching past
grass lands
and heifer-spotted
landscapes

road signs
promise
moose – elk – deer
eyes peeled
for
big-footed men
for our reflections
in stone

emotional
ups and downs
crowned at
toothy summits
sliver wide highways
balanced
between

judgment and progress

referendum deals
gone dead
stirred up
deep beds
laid to rest
new relationships
of silence
and inertia

these lands
grow and recede
and always
teach
us ways
to get around
shows us where
the trails lead

to live
in this land
you must understand
real histories
still lived

No, that's not
a ski slope
that's a mountain
we pray there.

HOME-MADE BOOZE

with expert F-X
minds sent spinning winging
through space
at hellish pace
falling   *splat cold*
against brick
tenement homes
where young ones play

cascade

down monkey bar mountains
too high slides
and rubble stone

in streets
brown brothers meet
passing liquid stories
over garbage can heat
gathered in wind-chilled circles

butter-ball dreams
tease
single mom
while rent is due
Home-made booze
of government bread
and orange juice
consumed

Happy Thanksgiving prayers

reach ears
of autumn coloured
spirits
secretly
placing
ten cent pieces
along well worn paths
for the small ones

busted but not broken
the people carry on

INTO SPIRIT

he passed through gates
opened by his will
entered a grassland
peaceful *quiet*
heaven's doors folded closed
behind him
leaving a green globe spinning
slow constant

he sat by a fire and told it
his stories
the flame grew and receded
in response to his talk
the heat absorbed all his confessions
relieving him of his burdens

the stars appeared as stairs
leading upward
to the unknown
he rose
to a place of suspension
reflection stillness
a child choir singing
songs for him
and him alone

he found his home
where he learns to make things grow

family friends
encircle him
radiating love
bringing him along
their son
my father
into Spirit

OPEN HEARTS

it is fast
like the passing
of seconds
its heat
is the fire
of beginning's
creation
passions
reaching heavens
our love
making
waves
into the universe
as joy
bright colours
blast through
clouds
reeling in
reluctant feelings

absence and
meditations
communications
with spirit
we call them
down
with winged
limbs
they fan
our flame
proving
two is one
separation undone
a marriage
of souls

hearts open
like the door
of a lodge
newness
distress
the unfamiliar
letting go
the powerful
greatness

you are the bird
I am the branch
you are the ear
I am the song
together
we make something
that doesn't look
like life
as we know it
it doesn't fit
into a box
or a house
it is wonder
and magnificence

it is laughter
and sorrow
we kick its ass
and it feeds us more
we enter
and recoil
it is the love
that is
us

LOVE AFFAIR – NOUNS

prayers
thoughts
words
wishes

gifts
friends
cups
clothing

telephone
poetry
dreams
destiny

dinner
winter
rings
promises

nothing but the Grand Master Plan
can bring two hearts together in honesty and trust

nothing but love can withstand
natural trials and tribulations of two hearts as they journey together

nothing would be left to discover
if you knew who your heart was to meet

nothing

absolutely nothing can write a heartfelt love poem
like a lost love wondering lonely looking for its mate

nothing

LOVE AFFAIR – VERBS

writing
waiting
resolving
wondering

moving
growing
dancing
understanding

speaking
listening
kissing
loving

living
coming
going
...returning

we wait for time to change the things we ourselves cannot

we wait to see what time brings to us

we wait too long for others to make up our minds and shape our lives

we wait and wonder what would have been

love does not wait

it offers itself and if rejected does not hang around for its own funeral

TRANSFUSION

cozied up content
against your bear skin stomach
listening as large vacuumous inhales
begin the story telling

muscles tighten slightly
your voice takes on
sharper tones quicker pace
as memory dictates

tales of a time
when men only had men
fight or fall
check the play
day after day after
live long day

survival instincts from inside
I listen wide-eyed
no judgment still content
to know of battles
the brethren wars
some did not live to tell

verbal spells spill into me
like blood dripping from a bag
transfusion stories
oral bloodletting
leaving you born new

it is you
inside me
tales reproducing themselves
blood cells
traveling
to the centre
of my heart

GO WEST

the snow fell heavy
over Montreal
blanketing city cement
muffling midways
and tightening collars
of passing pedestrians

her buildings were built
to withstand conditions
stinging snows biting sun
and everything
in between

the Basilica's bells
wave goodbye and cry
out songs of a sad yesterday
old altars stand precarious
hold loose prayers
the salt of tears
have eaten away their strength

the city waits on warmer days
for the last of polluted ice
to drain
for the crocuses to poke up
brave buds to break through
confirming changing seasons

Montreal embraces those
true of heart thick of skin
a people beaten not broken
she sings her proud songs
wearing gowns with tattered hems

it's hard work
keeping her face lifted
while only those gifted
with her language
understand
the original plan
is not what it is now

she needs snow cold
knowing it can preserve her

copper-topped roofs protrude
through a brown-grey landscape
to say

Hey! We still have soul.

the snow falls heavy
over Montreal
well into night
not even daylight savings
could make it stop

Pardonnez-moi – Arete
C'est ce la place pour

Onkwehonwe*

*Iroquois People

maple syrup souvenirs
Indians with accents
five day trampoline trip
just west-jet me home
where salt lives
in oceans
songs are trumpeted
from forests old
and mountains
do not host crosses
shining down
lit up like trees
at Christmas

SECOND LAST OF HER CLAN

I found her there
in the massive library
memories and evidence
of events both celebrated and tragic
pleased and frustrated
at the mystery she created
buried with her *finger to lips*
the faithful friends
and perplexed inspectors
let go the private life
of a flamboyant socialite
performer poet
living in at least *two worlds*
spanning *two land masses*
making friends and allies
and impressing the pants off
those who expected much less

her avant-garde recitals
left a dramatic impression
commanded serious questions
of rookie interviewers
while she was *who she was*
a beautiful fusion
of olive-skinned complexion
speaking in tongues and tones
acting as her own
passport into homes and concert halls
bringing with her trinkets
costume and gown
now lying in a town
she adopted
as home

Leaving no human legacy behind *she died*
second last of her clan
while the dedicated
honour her
the inspiration she gifted a nation

it was hard work being her *as honesty is*
destiny fulfilled Pauline E.
your sleep is well deserved

SAGE ADVICE

Loopholes are meant to be broken

Granny would get all the clichés wrong
but dispense them
like sage advice
to anyone
who cared to listen

A finger in time, saves nine
Step on a crack, you can't get it back

when I was twenty-two
I asked Granny

Why do you always get it wrong?

she looked at me
with black raccoon eyes
leaned in close
and took the flesh of my ear
between her bony fingers

she whispered

I know things, you don't
I've done things
and survived
things you pussy-spoiled
tit-sucking brat-ass kids
could never survive

she released me
and finished

That's why!

Now run along before
I kick you in the
Cha-boom

YOU KNOW ME

you know me
I know   you know me
show me   you know me
in front of god
and all these people here
see me   acknowledge me
put your game face on
and
approach me

shake my hand
if you dare   I dare you
I know you
yes   in that way
I know what you look like
in the dark
and I know
the people
you know

its okay
they can see   how
we know each other
fact is   I've known you
from a lifetime ago
and I know   you know me
from then too
so question is…
now that
you know me
do you
remember me
from then?

will we do it all again
next time around

or ignore the truth
turn on your boot
and pretend
like you don't know me

ROMANTIC INDIAN LOVE POEM

bring me spring water
to wash over my
tight skin

wrap me in birch bark
and peel me slow

be my canoe
let me ride you to
shore

take this leather lace
let your imagination
run wild

I'll feed you a bowl
of berries
and sing you old songs

heal me with strong tea
made of thistles and thorns

take me
into your lodge
let our love
light the fire

lay me down
on bear skin
brush me with sage

I will braid your hair
so we will never part

whisper to me
your animal spirit
and I will do the same

dream of warm winds
as I breathe into your ear

catch me a fish
from the morning stream
I'll cool you
with a feather fan
in the noon day sun

wear this string of beads
long enough to touch
your heart

together we'll grow old
with each passing season and moon

wrap me in a shawl
in the winter of my years

we'll send our arrows high
and catch us a star

when Creator calls to us
we'll approach
heads bent
and remember
berries, birch bark
and braids

I'll tell you stories
of love

from our place
in the sky

I WANT

your skin
is the kind
I like
right
colour
right
texture
reminds me
of
a fighter
gone
nine
wild rounds
and wins

your skin
brown
to beat
the band
smooth
like you
talking
to me
on the phone

take it off
let me see
what's
underneath
stand
right there
warm air
covers you

my eyes
devour you
your perfume
stays
with me
hours
afterwards

bring
your skin
to me
close
enough
to touch
but deny
me
one minute
more

now
cover it up
god's gift
you are
perfection
human creation
in
natural
light

you make me

want

you

HOT PLUMES

I saw two ravens kissing
high on the branch
of a bare naked tree
beaks touching
lightly fluffing
breaking their beautiful
union to caw romance
to one another
pledging togetherness
in song

Mr. and Mrs. Raven
cared not about the snow
bordering them or the cold
for they had hot plumes
tight holds on each other
and tiny bird hearts
beating faster with each kiss
so pure was their love act
I could not turn my gaze
but secretly assigned them names
after you and me

for we are like those ravens
high on each other
able to perch in suspended time
withstanding uncomfortable conditions
with the ability to see
far across lands
Lady Raven me
Master Raven you
kissing raven kisses
as full moon rises
blessing the night
its magic light
casting midnight spells

GRIZZLY BEAR MAN

you make me wanna

lock lips
swing hips

feed you black berries
from between my breasts

eat ice cream
two tongues
one cone

call you on the phone
make you cum long distance

hum blues tunes
into your ear
right here
on the pillow
we share

then   dance in the moonlight
like fire light
flickering our joy

oh boy

wanna transform
ten pounds
into sweat
by acts of
lust and passion and fun

then let the sun
blanket us like newborns
new forms
of union

sprung up
like daisies

you make me wanna

yes you do…

AROUND THE BEND ALONG THE BOW

river banks
lined with coloured memories
we bring shallow understanding
of your significance
release to you in trust
our hopes
for tomorrow

a people's heavy wanting
passes through liquid gates
transforms to foam   collecting
precarious   wishes
breathing   breaking
away

moody currents
turn to torrents
ragged rocks
cut smooth skins
revealing rough beds

impatient spring flows
kiss icy shoulders
the magic melting
widens your capacity
to grant our blue desires

wait for the babies
for the buds and lovers
to mark your holy platforms
dipping innocently
in your baptismal waters
caressing   soothing
the saddest of souls
with energy-filled
fluid vibrations

changing directions
you keep us guessing
rising   receding
femme fatale

deep enough
to be dangerous
long enough
to carry us away
making graves
for our ashes
and abandoned dreams
for all things left behind

we
follow
you
in
time

NO KISS GOODBYE

when you left
there was no kiss goodbye
only eyes
reflecting back
this was our end
this was me finishing
with you
saving myself
from your torment
as you turned away
there was no blame
you came in
your soupy state
so thick the drugs
swam through
your sedated veins
and everything
was thrown out the window

I'm so glad
you're gone
I'm so happy
to be done
and that you
did away
with yourself
not even animals
continue to suffer so
and the dope
and vile acts
you could not take back
brought you to that place

there was no kiss goodbye
only understanding
of what needed to be done
and pictures
a handsome fleshy face
looking back
brave and broken
I can see my tomorrow
and choose to live
making the commitment
you could not
to complete happiness

breathe in your spirit life
with peace
and Divine Love

our time
was horrible and good
and perfect

no kiss goodbye

required

FLAG SONG

hot drum
tight-skinned toned
tiny pulse grows
into our souls
wailing vocal throat
ancient broken notes
wind inspired scream
I weep
I weep

Grandfather voice crack
flag song pride
brought back
through time tracks
Saulteaux remix
born to live again
drum beat heart beat
internal cleansing spells
leaving only shells
weak in the presence
of spirit strong
flag song

young ones stand tall
with rich lineage
granted and bestowed
claim their place
strong shouldered soldier
warrior of the plains

rhythm commands my blood
to pulse
and tears to fall in line
ancestor memory
surfacing to earth
Blood love
Blood love

sing the language
honour by prayer
frozen in time
fusing our hearts into one

faster chants
accent beats
raising spirits
fiery screech

medicines

drum medicines
recovered from old
precious as gold
pricey all the same
standing circle
ringing tones
haunted hearts
held in love

ancestor song sung

medicines

drum medicines

born to live again
born to live again

THE LAST FLOOD

in a land
with tricky water
reserves
sand bags at the ready
waiting to sop up
emotional messes
legacies
left by churches
threat of floods
permeate the air
spins prickly electricity
over unsuspecting vegetation

while winter snows
melt in spring
heavy water falls
speed and tear
away protective rock layers
revealing soft brown clay
of the original people

pre-contact people

pre-broken heart people

before removal
before numerous losses
too many to mention

dams burst open
and confuse the fish
all hell breaks loose
in memory floods
uncontrollable currents
rising levels spill into
innocent territory
unnatural acts
nature
out of its
element
painful
and
pleasurable

Chaos

families can only wait
for levels to subside
leaving once hard lands
weepy   waiting
for heat   evaporation

new crusts will form

new life will be born

memories of generations
long gone down river
songs sung in honour

harmonies linger
repeating
resounding as
echoes
reminding us
of the last
flood